Roman Soldier

Baby

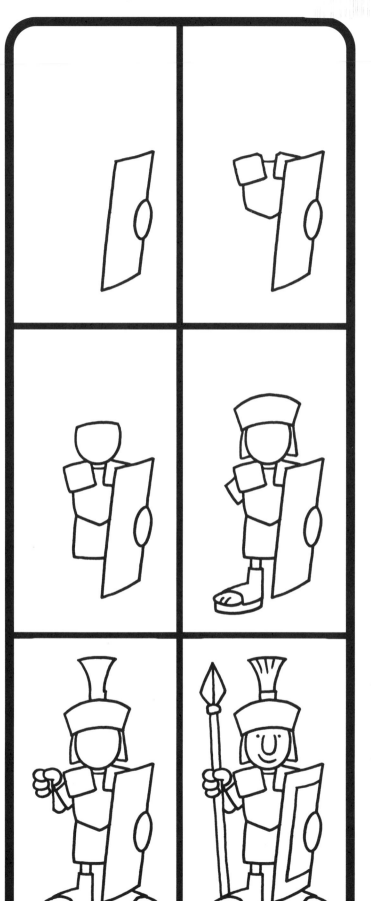

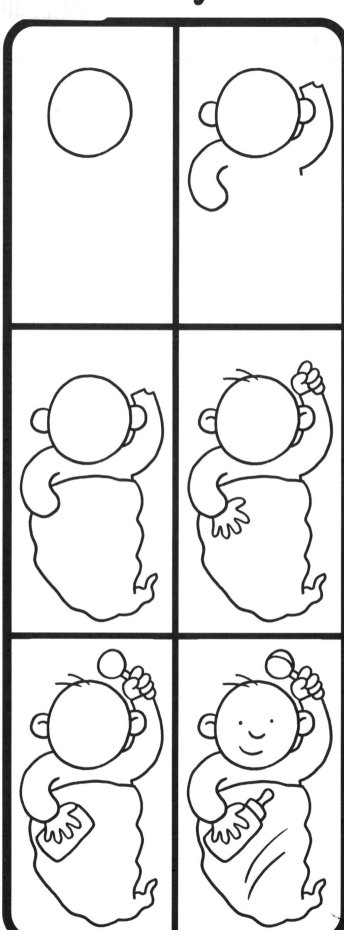

In-line Skater

Mechanic

Astronaut

School Girl

King

Queen

Doctor

African Musician

Mum

Dad

Brother

Sister

Gran

Grandad

Pharaoh

Clown

Skateboarder

Greek Scholar

Cowboy

Flamenco Dancer

Toddler

Judge

Greek Soldier   Victorian Lady

Teddy Boy

Teacher

Black Belt

Sailor

Tennis Player   Builder

Bride

Father Christmas

Roman Emperor

Nurse

opera Singer

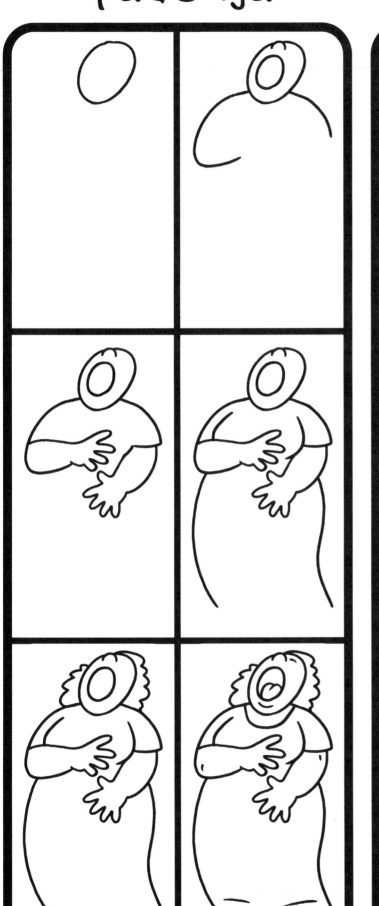

Sheriff

Artist

Witch

Dentist

Football Player

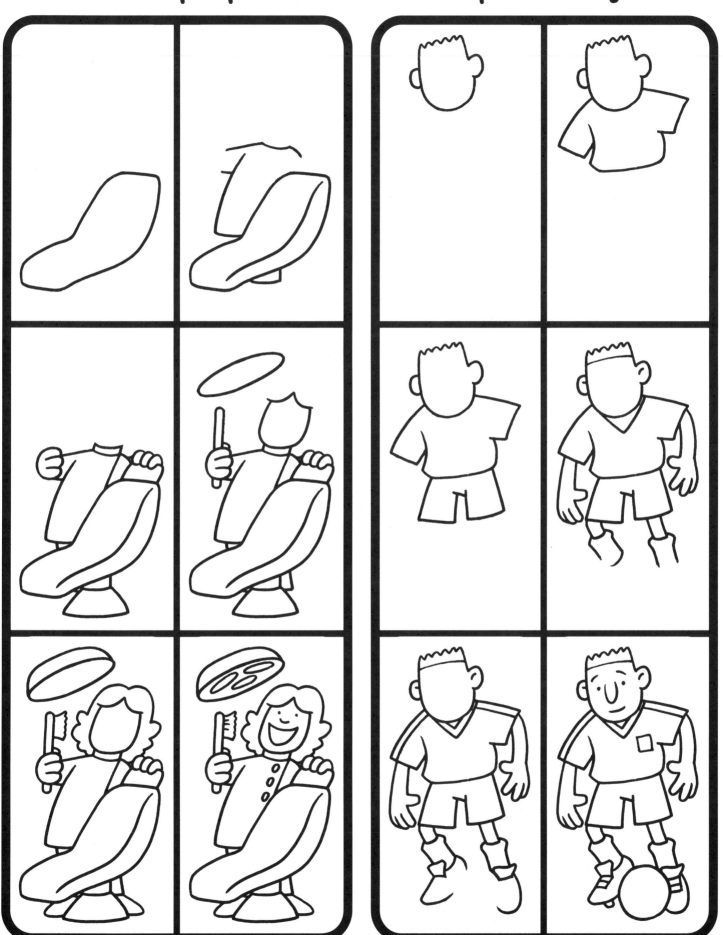

Ice Skater

Superhero

Diver

Burglar

Chef

Elf

Cave Woman

Cave Man

Gardener

Baseball Player

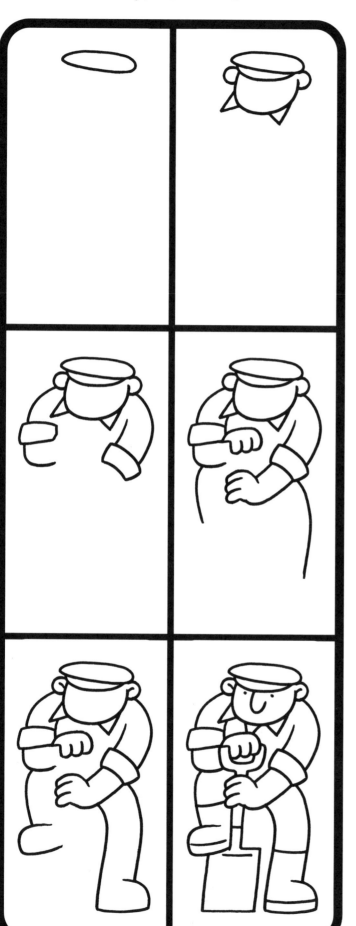

Fairy   # Baker

Tightrope Walker

Fisherman

Magician

Knight

Policeman

BMX

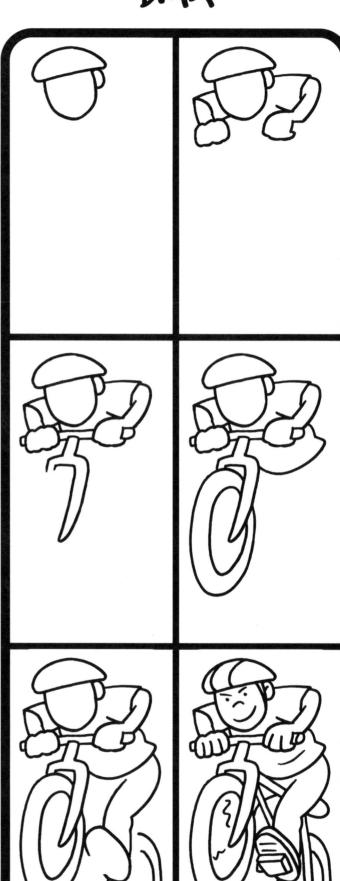

Rock'n'Roll Dancer

Postman

Inuit   Scuba Diver

Fireman

Arab

Hippy   Lumberjack

Emperor

Indian Dancer

Victorian Gentleman   Ballet Dancer

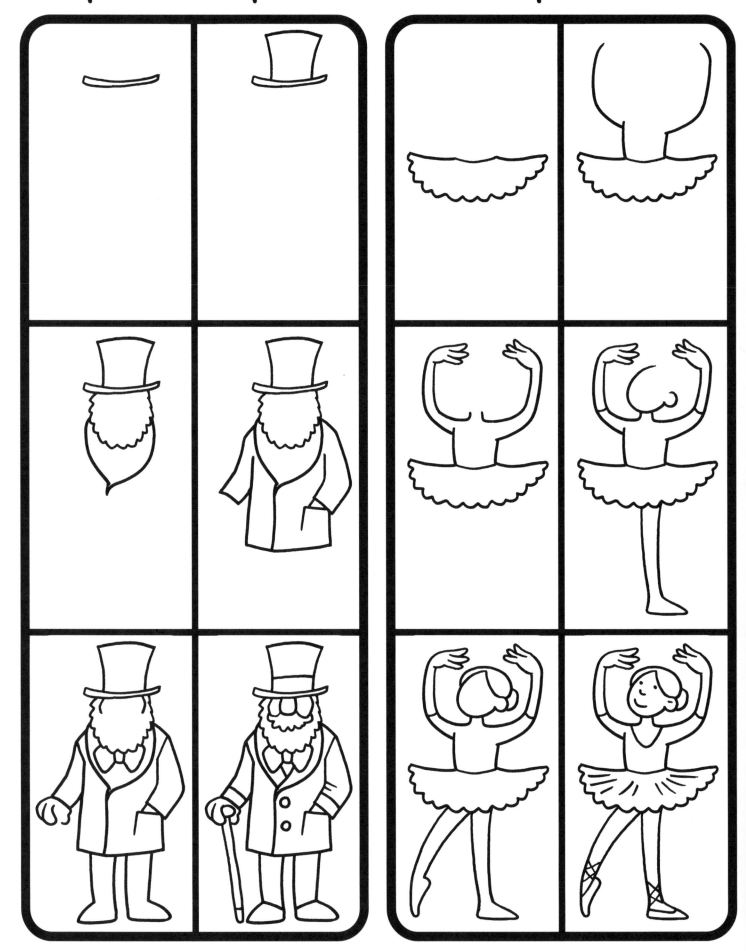

Painter

Farmer

Viking

Jump

Skip

1970s Pop Star

Actor

Handstand

Surgeon   Chinese Lady

Scientist

Butcher

Pirate   Mountaineer

Deep Sea Diver

Wizard

Captain

Dwarf

Tarzan

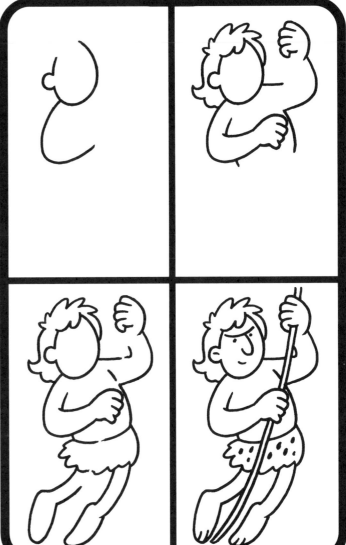

Skier

Surfer

Vicar

High Jumper

Weightlifter

Juggler

Conductor

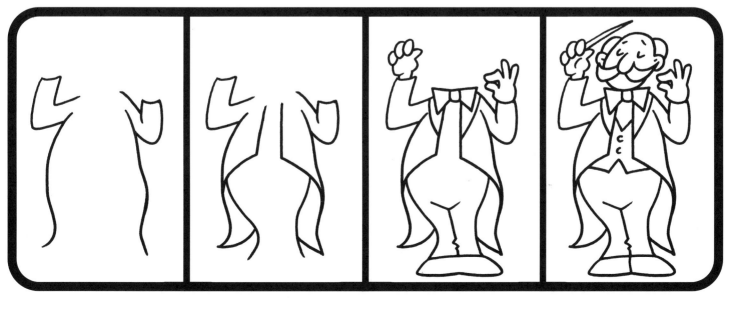

Basketball Player

Waiter

American football Player

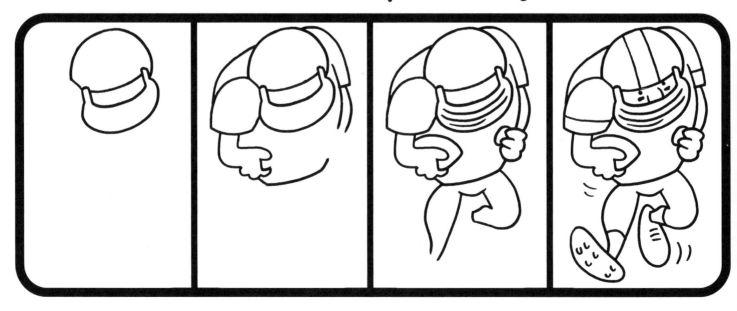